DONE THAT

POETRY & POSICS

Written and Performed
by
Paula Curci

A special thanks goes out
to those who have participated
in this project and have…
<u>Been There and Done That!</u>

Zoe - Jade Austin
Kiki Calafell
Christopher Carroll
Donna Carroll
Frank X. Curci
Lucy Curci-Gonzalez & Family
Gary Duff
Nassau County Poet Laureate Society
Peyton Pleninger
Christine Ranieri
James Romano
Theresa Rosario-Berzner
Mike Sapone
Emilio Squillante III
Tullio Vacchio
WRHU Radio Hofstra University
John Zych

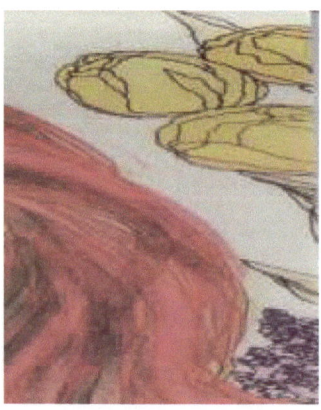

© 2022 Paula Curci All Rights Reserved

Copyright © 2022 PAULA CURCI

ALL RIGHTS RESERVED

No part of this publication may be copied, reproduced, modified, altered, republished, or distributed in any form, or by any means, or included or stored in any other publication, data base, retrieval system, or any other media (now known or developed in the future) without the prior written permission of Paula Curci.

The **POSICS**™ trademark,
the **ACOUSTIC POETS NETWORK**™ trademark, and
the **WHAT'S THE BUZZ**® trademark
(Collectively the "Marks")
are owned by Paula Curci and all rights are reserved in all such Marks.

Some of the poems in this chapbook have been separately registered with the United States Copyright Office and such copyrights are owned by Paula Curci.

Some of the poems in this chapbook can also be found digitally or in print in previously published works or anthology compilation literary reviews.

Some of the poems in this collection were previously performed or distributed by and/or through the use of the **ACOUSTIC POETS NETWORK**™ trademark and brand.

ISBN 978-0-9654831-5-5
Printed in the USA

The following poems are written and created by Paula Curci.

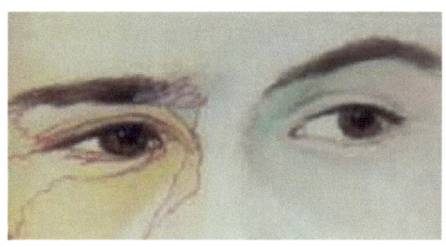

TABLE OF CONTENTS

MEETING CALLIOPE	5
True Women	7
You Are Gonna Find Out	8
Puck — A Midsummer Warning	10
MOVE OVER	11
Jack n' Jill	12
Juliet's Words	14
WAITING	15
Virginia	16
Spaghetti Western	17
Ocean Ride Noir	18
LONG BEACH MYSTERY	19
Buried In the Earth…Part One	21
Buried in the Dirt…Part Two	22
Been There	24
Done That	25
Robert Or What Roads Diverge in My Soul?	26
My Awakening: Rumi with Tabla	27
CREDITS	28
LINER NOTES	29
ABOUT THE AUTHOR	31

MEETING CALLIOPE

Around the corner this page I meet a cool Greek woman who mused that hell out of some really important Gods and Goddesses. She told me not to worry about Samuel Coleridge or T.S. Eliot or Charles Bukowski; not to worry about the job clever young poets have, because anyone who wonders about young poets must be old.

She told me that being old does not mean you are wise and that being an American does not mean that you are wise and that speaking English does not mean that you are wise and liking football, cars, hot dogs, does not mean you are wise. Cause wisdom could be found in a chocolate peppermint girl scout cookie. Cause wisdom could be found in the knot that ties your hammock to your tree. Cause wisdom is found in the nature you grow around you.

Once I finally shook my head letting her know that I got the picture she told me that she was older than old, she was Aniee, an elder, because she was anno mundo, born in the beginning of the world and that since I was a woman who was younger than she I would always be a young poet. So of course, this made me feel good and I continued to listen to this sage and she went on to tell me all sorts of adventures about c'est la vie and she continued to talk about c'est la guerre.

She began to talk so fast I was getting confused and I stopped and protested. "Not all things should be accepted just because they are." I said, "Aren't there any new profound things your Gods have shared with you while you stole sad moments from them with your epic poetry?"

"Au contraire!" She said, "En re'gle, en re'gle- in due time … deeds are males' words are females. That is why I am a poet. I am a woman." She told me, "And patience comes from time and time makes one wise and the voice of the poet is the voice of the people and the voice of the people is the voice of Gods."

And since she mused a few, I knew that this was the best advice she could give this young poet.

Signed, Corner

True Women

True women are distribution centers,
talking to one another,
telling their sons' stories
and instructing these to be kings
just like Lemuel's mother.

True women
struggle through harvest,
sharing truth,
prospering within to bear down
and meet with their bibles Ruth.

True women
are stewards of love,
showering energy,
embracing their faith
like Queen Esther did for his majesty.

True women
wait for due season,
standing ready,
choosing what is best.
Living proof
that mistake can be forgiven,
by making room for their enemy
to be their guest.

You Are Gonna Find Out

It's gonna happen
one day you gonna wake up
walk out the door
and find out it ain't the same
way as it was before
As it shoulda been, coulda been
da da da da da da

Don't know what to tell ya
But the Outer Banks could be gone tomorrow
And community could be full of sorrow
Next week saint Helen Could blow
people just won't
know what to do where to go
worst of all it's all happened before
we know the score
that earthquake blasted
it was forecasted
and that hurricane that split up Able and Cain
they wrote about that
even planned a whole format
for evacuation and rehabilitation
and the peace keepers who brought on the grim reapers
they couldn't afford chaos or accord
since it exists in each of us
their sins grew tedious

So, what could we do but look toward you?
and walk in unison
and find faith in something
and rely on the little bita good
from those in our own neighborhood

So, when you stride into the world to find out

Look out
yea things are gonna change some
ya gotta have a little more
ya gotta have a little more
you gotta have a little more
faith in something

Cause one day its gonna to happen
ya gonna wake up
walk out the door
and find out
it ain't the same way as it was before
shoulda been, coulda been
da da da da da
don't know what to tell
you gotta have faith in something

Puck — A Midsummer Warning

There is always a Puck
who drops a thunderstroke
one who does another's bidding
and waits for further treasure.
There is always a Puck
lurking in two dimensions
lowering wicked spirits and madness
for granted fortune future.
There is always a Puck.
He lives unfree, shaded by rock.
He will jest with you,
all that lies beneath the stars can shine.
Recall he is a jest,
fast and quick with the nuances of language.
Take good aim at his features
the lines across his face
each slow syllable
each action taken.
I've told in short
by the passing of the sun
after the night sleeps
beware of the Puck!

MOVE OVER

Move over, move over, something's taken over …

People on the left are stepping over all the people on the right
and vice versa and those in the middle, lost in the riddle,
they're not sleeping at night.

You know we could go to the farm stand and buy a new
cherry pie.
If we buy it frozen, we can save a little bit of money.
And honey, in these times we need to save some money.

I'm still waiting for best new folk song to wake us up.
Cause Arlo has been long gone and Dylan, he's willing to play,
but he's in Hempstead charging for a forty-dollar parking pass.

Move over, move, over something's taken over...

In this land of constant sorrow,
a few new folk songs need to come, tomorrow,
cause John Henry sold his hammer a long time ago.

I'm still waiting for folk music with a beat.
Cause Tom Dooley is still alive walking the street
and Sylvie can't find clean water.

I'm still looking for the Mary Ellen Carter to rise again
and I'm still looking for the Mary Ellen Carter to rise again.

Move over, move over, something's taken over…

Jack n' Jill

Jack and Jill went up the hill to fetch a pail of water.
Jack fell down and broke his crown
and Jill
she's left with a pocket full of posies
a room filled with roses
and ashes and ashes
cause he fell down.
You see, Jack was supposed to be nimble.
Jack was supposed to be quick.
Jack wasn't supposed to fall down.
and Jack wasn't supposed to get sick,

And the rain, the rain
the rain, rain won't go away
it's here to stay day by day
and the only thing I can hear her say is:

"Rain on the green grass
rain on the trees
rain on the rooftops
but
stop raining on me
pull the petals
pull the petals
he loves me
he loves me not
he loves me
he loves me not
you're supposed
to be here
but you're not!"

Now there goes little woman, little jumping Jill.
Now that Jacks gone, wonder how she'll get her fill.
As I heard the story to keep,
little Jill went to the market when Jack was asleep.
As I heard the story to tell,

she went to the market when he fell
and home went little woman,
poor little Jill,
Old woman now living under a hill.
Old woman tossed in a basket,
whose love lives in a casket.
Old woman who lives in a shoe,
tell me, what's she to do?

Old women, you must stand still,
still, in the garden
where Mary's garden grows
those roses of red
those violets of blue.
And Jill,
the woman standing still,
still cries…

"Rain on the green grass
rain on the trees
rain on the rooftops
but
stop raining on me
pull the petals
pull the petals
he loves me
he loves me not
he loves me
he loves me not
you're supposed
to be here,
but you're not.

You're supposed
to be here,
but you're not!"

Juliet's Words

What dreams are these,
talking with eyes closed?
Private and stolen pictures of love,
like an opera,
swaying with the power of language.
I will not cry,
I have a place in this Kingdom.
Even if Shakespeare brings on the line,
I will not die for you, Romeo.
Romeo, wherefore art thou Romeo?
I will not die for you, Romeo.
You thought more of yourself than I.
You Romeo,
failed to check my pulse!

<u>WAITING</u>

Oh, what power the gift he gives us
to see ourselves as others see us.
Why don't you spend this time with me?
Here,
under this orange sky,
I am Gadot.
Waiting.
Now that my necklace of love and loyalty,
has been released from your mind,
I am not comforted by that vision.
You have stolen Mark Twains' shadow off the
Mississippi,
only to leave me here dancing, with Ophelia.
As my love clashes,
I am kicking up Angela's ashes,
an indigo girl
blue around the skin.
I want the gift he gave us,
to see ourselves as others see us.
Why don't you spend this time with me?

Virginia

Virginia, Virginia
Wake up now Virginia
Wake up, listen up Virginia.
They are lying to you Virginia.
Just put yourself in pause,
cause there ain't no Santa Claus,
no shooting stars,
no fairy grandma.
Wake up!
When I snap my fingers twice,
don't matter if
you're naughty or your nice,
just throw out that tooth instead,
Virginia.
Cause no fairy
is going to visit you in bed!

Spaghetti Western

It was late October in Wyoming.
Sarah Pinkerton,
sensing his restlessness,
has been pleading with Jed Clayton
to settle down with her.
After tenderly drying her eyes,
Jed turns to her and says:
"I got a horse and the west is wide.
I need a place where I can ride.
You know like I do friends do change.
I gotta live out on the range.
I gotta ranch and a cattle hand
and you got away with the city land.
You know like I do, the two don't mix.
I gotta go, for it needs to be fixed.
We hear the loud Calgary bugles calls;
we hear the shots and the cannon balls.
You know like I do,
when there is a hole in the wall,
I gotta gallop before I fall.
So, let's sing good bye songs while we sit.
Let's wet our eyes for just a bit.
So, bye for now,
I'm saddling up.
Leaving you,
with the big sheep dog pup.
Remember me when the credits roll,
my big heart and my roaming soul.
Cause what I need is a place to ride.
I got a horse and the west is wide.
Cause what I need is a place to hide.
I got a horse and the west is wide.
I got a horse and the west is wide.
I got a horse and the west is wide."

Ocean Ride Noir

I can see the point of the needle ahead,
driving toward Gatsby
and just before Zach's Bay,
I'll take my exodus there.
I have an appointment.
Somewhere mid-island.
I am past due.
In nine months
the weather will clear
and top downs - will open.
But right now,
I've got to clear that roundabout
It's still dark out.
The fog is low
and thank God for this arabica joe,
it's keeping me steady.
As thunder roars on this ocean road
the chilled, thick air,
doesn't stop the biker's riding.
They're helmet clad,
with knee and elbow pads
ready for the fall.
I no longer see the needle,
It vanishes in my rear view.
Driving across the bridge,
leaving the desert behind me
I am racing against time,
against the tide.
I'm meeting up with my destiny.
Like Moses,
I just can't let them catch up with me.

LONG BEACH MYSTERY

In years past Long Beach was a sleepy cottage resort where windows were covered with bronze wire cloth in the summer and wood boards in the Winter. Doors swung in the spring and creaked in the fall. But in the odd ides of March unsolved mysteries lingered between the slats of each wooden beach fence that separated the walks from the sand.

These stories were unearthed on grey sodden Saturdays in March, where their characters woke to meet on the melancholy sand dunes that manifested between the winter and the spring dimensions. Once released from their chambers, the ghosts rose and floated over the beach grass. The guilty and the innocent lingered on opposite sides of each other to repeat a court like ritual that ended each time with a jury's thunder, in the wind. The culpable were left exposed on the cold sand to reveal their transparent skin, waterlogged by years of evil.

On that day nameless boys stood undaunted, theatrically posing Napoleon-like, with one arm on their chest while the others waved unlit cigars chanting "innocent, innocent" into the breeze. They had no notion that they were chained in this evil loop for eternity, indicted by their victims in this perdition.

Tired and wounded, Lewis Edwards limped between the ocean's foam to greet the starlet, Star Faithful. Just off the Mauritania, in her black and white dress with seaweed in her hair. He took her hand; they were both barristers on this judgement day. In their final summation, he spoke of her regrets; she shared his efforts for reform.

Since the faithful new who was guilty and since poltergeist were only heard in dreams or drafts, she spoke into the wind. She said, "I know who done it."

If you listen closely on a stormy Saturday in March, in the city by the sea, you can hear an echo as it drifts through the air. It's the judgement of the phantom jury. "We know who done it, we know who done it."

Buried In the Earth…Part One

I've been working with the earth.
Moving dirt around, like clay.
Making space for stones,
and ditches for drains.
Last night I dreamt
I was coffined,
underground.
Crunching mud
and fear of Covid,
has me thinking
of my mortality.
Has me scrubbing my nails,
and scratching…
my way out of dreams.

Buried in the Dirt…Part Two

Channeling Edgar Allen Poe,
April showers can be heard
the hard hail clouds let
the grass soak and get
the seeds to stick for the heron.
She flies here and parks
near the Usher house,
quiet as a mouse.
But I hear pitter patter…
a knocking so loud,
like one on the door.
'It's not real', I swore!
And began to rake and load.

On earth or under,
stab life with the blade,
when you're channeling Edgar,
doesn't matter where you've laid.

Gather the shovels
and level the ground!
My heart still pounds,
as I push and shake…
this monster like thought,
this bad night dreaming.
Remove its meaning!
Bring on a spring like thinking.
Changing the image,
of telltale sounding,
my knuckles pounding.
Instead, flowers should emerge

On earth or under,
stab life with the blade,
when you're channeling Edgar,
doesn't matter where you've laid.

Can't control my departure,
but I can pull up bad roots
and harvest sweet fruits.
First, I have a chore to do
destroy these shoots!

Been There
(A seven syllable-double Rondelle)

You have met me here before.
Sometime in the last century,
around some visionary,
before climate change and Gore.

We danced on this very floor,
with cheer, in bright light merry,
with lively esprit de corps.
Then things got a bit heavy.

After the cabaret law,
going to the library
was simply mandatory.
Sighting Rumi and Tagore
or Utopia by More

The salon was less a bore.
The writing community,
lost with opportunity,
became new troubadours.

In the San Francisco store
with the Hippies and Jali,
mixing his beat poetry
and her stories of folklore.

Words, they are communal core
so clear, it's necessary.
They're made the same, but vary.
Some things we cannot ignore.
We have all been here before!

Done That

So, they say
they don't need understanding.
I get it very well.
Been There – Done That.
Not everyone can heed warning
from someone else's tell.

No need in comprehending.
Let someone be there
or help when landing
naked and bare.
I spit that phlegm,
cleaned up those messes,
tried to tell them,
have less guesses.
But not everyone hears.
They just catch edges,
clinging to tears
and hanging off ledges.

So, they say
it's not the same.
I know that very well.
Been There- Done That.
Old story, new name.
All those tales we all tell.

Robert
Or
<u>What Roads Diverge in My Soul?</u>

What roads diverge in my soul of love and desire,
to travel on a wooded road,
to make camp and read poetry by a warm fire?
I've told people I'm a counselor,
a craftsman of words.
But who is it that really knows me,
when alone in the wood with the birds?
Somewhere my future Robert will return
and in this weary soul of mine, his ideas will churn.
As my mornings begin to equal that of his,
I will recognize the undergrowth,
with a knowing
that…this is the way it is.

And I will slow down
on this road
that I've traveled on
so fast.

My Awakening: Rumi with Tabla

With Rumi's
spirit at my side,
I woke this
Morning.
The sun filtered
and light reached my eyes,
desire reached my body,
dreaming.
Rumi sang with a Reed
telling stories of life,
stories of liberty,
a tale of love,
and the pursuit of happiness.
In this early dawn of happiness
he whispered the sun,
he whispered the stars,
a tale of the moon
and he gave me golden kisses.
Love fire tangled in reed notes
sang from my bed.
Longing for your face this,
passion evoked flames
and I kissed Rumi
good morning.

CREDITS

The DONE THAT project includes both this chapbook and the digital version of Paula Curci's Poetry and **POSICS™** performances and works.

The DONE THAT project embraces the found and cento poem form, cover versions, and references to other songwriters and poets who have "done that" along the way. The poems included in DONE THAT represent the cycles of life. It reflects on the stories we have all lived through. It acknowledges that we've all "been there" at one time or another.

This chapbook includes seventeen poems. There is also an audio version of this work that is presented in Paula's spoken word **POSICS™** style of work --- and in that audio version there are nineteen poems, including the seventeen printed here.

The poem by Shakespeare, "Sonnet #18", and the poem by Edgar Allan Poe, "The Happiest Day", are performed by Paula on the digital version of DONE THAT and are not printed in this chapbook.

Some of the poems in this chapbook can also be found digitally or in print in previously published works and/or anthology compilation literary reviews.

Some of the poems in this collection were previously performed and/or distributed by or through the use of Paula's **ACOUSTIC POETS NETWORK** ™ trademark and brand.

LINER NOTES

— Kiki Calafell ©1995

The following is a list of contributors to the audio version of this work

Sonnet 18 – Words by William Shakespeare.
Music by Mike Sapone
Happiest Day – Words by Edgar Allen Poe.
Music by Mike Sapone
Jack n' Jill – Music by Tullio Vacchio
Waiting Music – Music by John Zych
Spaghetti Western – Music adapted by John Zych
Intro Voiced by Zoe-Jade Austin
Virginia SFX adapted by John Zych
Your Gonna Find Out – Music by Christopher Carroll
Long Beach Mystery – SFX by Christopher Carroll
Ocean Ride – SFX adapted by Christopher Carroll
Been There – Saxophone by Peyton Pleninger
My Awakening with Tabla – Music by Christopher Carroll
Engineers: Christopher Carroll, Mike Sapone, John Zych

The art work in this chapbook, and in its audio version, was created and is owned by

Kiki Calafell.

All of her art work has been included herein with her permission:

"When I First Saw You" - Kiki Calafell ©1995
"Do You Remember?" - Kiki Calafell ©1995
The logo for the Acoustic Poets Network - Kiki Calafell ©1995

ABOUT THE AUTHOR

Paula Curci is the Nassau County (New York) Poet Laureate for 2022-2024. She is a spoken word poet, radio talk show host, and educator. Paula is a resident of Long Island, New York.

Paula is known for her poetry performance aesthetic that she has, for many years, called **POSICS™**.

POSICS™ is the trademark and brand that Paula uses to identify her style of spoken word that include recitations and singing, and her style of written works.

Paula produces "Calliope's Corner: The Place Where Poets and Songwriters Meet" and **WHAT'S THE BUZZ®** on WRHU 88.7fm Radio Hofstra University and WRHU.ORG. Her broadcasts have received numerous accolades, including a Gracie award and several Press Club of Long Island awards.

Her work as an educator has been honored by the March of Dimes and by the Nassau County School Counselor's Association.

As the co-founding member of the **ACOUSTIC POETS NETWORK™**, a group of poets who coordinate open mic events and formed a poetry band with the same name, Paula has produced, and owns the copyright in, two CD's entitled "Emissary" and" Bittersweet" which were released under the **ACOUSTIC POETS NETWORK™** trademark and brand.

Paula has also published, and owns the copyright in, two chapbooks entitled "One Woman's Cathartic Release in Poetry" and "The Gift of Thanksgiving."

Many of Paula's works have been published in various print anthologies and audio compilation music projects.

Several of Paula's works and performances are available for purchase on various digital sites.

Your QR Code to find
Done That: Poetry and Posics™
By Paula Curci and The Acoustic Poets Network™
The Audio Version
on Amazon!

www.ingramcontent.com/pod-product-compliance
Lightning Source LLC
Chambersburg PA
CBHW041912040426
42449CB00024BA/26